WILBUR & ORVILLE WRIGHT

Reference Edition Published 1988

Published by Marshall Cavendish Corporation
147 West Merrick Road
Freeport, Long Island
N.Y. 11520

Printed in Italy by New Interlitho, Milan.

Designed and produced by
AS Publishing

Library of Congress Cataloging-in-Publication Data

Wilbur & Orville Wright
        p. cm. − (Children of history; 5)
    Includes index.
    Summary: A biography concentrating on the childhood of the
airplane inventors Wilbur and Orville Wright.
    ISBN 0-86307-927-X. ISBN 0-86307-922-9 (set)
    1. Wright, Wilbur, 1867-1912−Juvenile literature. 2. Wright,
Orville, 1871-1948−Juvenile literature. 3. Aeronautics−United
States−Biography−Juvenile literature. H. Wright, Wilbur,
1867-1912−Childhood and youth. 2. Wright, Orville, 1971-1948−
−Childhood and youth.\3. Aeronautics−Biography.] I. Series:
Children of history; v. 5.
TL540.W7W7 1988
629.13'092'2−dc19
[B]
[920]

CHILDREN OF HISTORY

WILBUR & ORVILLE WRIGHT

By Theodore Rowland-Entwistle
Illustrated by W. Francis Phillipps

MARSHALL CAVENDISH
NEW YORK, LONDON, TORONTO

The Wright Brothers

Back at the beginning of the 20th century, traveling was slow and tedious. The automobile had only just been invented. If you had to make a long journey you went by train or by ship. Today, if you want to go on a long journey you probably fly in an airplane. The fact that you can do so is due to the vision and hard work of two brothers who lived and worked in Dayton, Ohio. Their names were Wilbur and Orville Wright.

On December 17, 1903, the Wright brothers made mankind's first flights in a powered airplane. Those flights were very short, lasting less than a minute. But they marked the beginning of the air age.

The Wright brothers never went to college or studied engineering, though Orville afterwards said that if they had done so it would probably have made their scientific work easier. But even when they were young they were always inventing or making things. One secret of their success was that they worked as a team.

Only five spectators saw the first powered flight on December 17, 1903. Few people realized what an important event had just taken place, and Wilbur Wright especially wanted to keep the brothers' invention secret until they had perfected it.

Each of the brothers was a fine craftsman, but together they developed an almost uncanny ability to solve problems. Also, they were good businessmen, and they were able to pay for their experiments themselves. The development costs for that first airplane – the *Flyer* – were less than $1,000. One of their rivals spent more than $50,000 trying to make a successful flying machine.

The Wright Family

The father of Wilbur and Orville Wright was a minister of the United Brethren Church, the Reverend Milton Wright. Milton went to a small college at Hartsville, Indiana, to study for the ministry. He was given a license to preach in 1846 when he was only 18 years old, but he decided to spend some time teaching before taking up his duties as a preacher.

On a visit back to Hartsville, young Milton met a bright, charming girl named Susan Catherine Koerner, who had been brought up on a farm.

Among other things, Susan was good at mathematics. From her father she inherited an ability to make and mend things. Most women in those days were expected to make and mend clothes, but Susan could also carry out what we would now call "do-it-yourself" jobs around the house.

Milton and Susan were married in 1859, about five years after they first met. Milton was just 31, and Susan was 28. They lived at several different places in Indiana where Milton was appointed as preacher. Like many other country clergymen, Milton seems also to have run a small farm from time to time.

Four Boys and a Girl

It was a noisy household that Wilbur and Orville grew up in. There were four boys and a girl in it. The eldest was Reuchlin, and he was followed by Lorin, a year younger. The two elder boys and Wilbur, who was five years younger than Lorin, were born in Indiana.

Soon after Wilbur's birth, on April 16, 1867, Milton Wright was appointed pastor back at his old college, Hartsville. But hardly had the family settled in than Milton

---

FATHER'S FAMILY
The Wrights were descended from an English ancestor, Samuel Wright, who emigrated to America in 1636, just 16 years after the Pilgrims. The family joined the United Brethren Church, which was was founded in America about 1755. It was a Protestant sect very like the Methodist Church in its beliefs, and since 1968 one section of the Church has been united with the Methodists.

MOTHER'S FAMILY
Susan Catherine Koerner was the daughter of John Koerner, an independent-minded German who had emigrated to Virginia in 1818 because he disliked the way the rulers of his own land behaved. John Koerner set up in business as a farmer and a builder of carriages and farm wagons. He married Catherine Fry, an American girl whose ancestors came from German-speaking Switzerland.

---

was made editor of *The Religious Telescope*, a church weekly newspaper. This meant another move, to Dayton, Ohio.

In Indiana the Wrights had lived in small towns. Dayton was a growing industrial city. Milton Wright was able to buy a new house, No. 7 Hawthorne Street, some distance from the main business district. There he and Susan settled down with their three boys. A year later, on August 19, 1871, Orville was born.

The Wright family: Kate, the youngest child, was her brothers' most loyal supporter when they were working on their aircraft.

There is no doubt that Wilbur was the more gifted of the two brothers, though Orville was always full of good ideas for earning money. He needed it – to repay his debts to Wilbur.

Will and Orv

Because Reuchlin and Lorin were so close in age, and so much older than Wilbur, they were almost like another family. Wilbur took his new brother under his wing, and as soon as Orville was old enough it seemed natural for the younger pair to play together, while Reuchlin and Lorin went off to school.

Orville did not stay the youngest for long. On his third birthday his mother produced a very special present for him: a baby sister. She was named Katharine, which was her mother's second name – though it was spelled differently. The little girl was always known as Kate, while Wilbur was Will to everybody, and Orville was Orv.

There were not so many toys for children sold in the stores in those days as there are now. People used to make many of their children's playthings. Both Milton and Susan were good at this, and as soon as he was old enough to use tools young Will, too, was whittling away at bits of wood to make things for himself and Orv.

Odd Jobs

The Reverend Milton Wright used to encourage his boys in their hobby of making things. He also persuaded them that if they needed money for a project they should try to earn it. So they did odd jobs and repairs around the house to help their mother. She paid them one cent every time they dried the supper dishes for her.

Although the two boys shared so many things, they were already developing different natures. Will was more inventive. He was careful to save some of the money he earned. Orv spent his money more quickly, so he used to have to borrow from Will to make ends meet.

A STARTING POINT
A gyroscope contains a heavy wheel mounted in a frame. The frame is free to move inside another frame, so the axle on which the wheel turns can point in any direction. When you set the wheel spinning the gyroscope will balance on a knife blade, or on a person's finger – and as long as the wheel stays spinning the gyroscope doesn't fall over.

The Gyroscope

Orville's fifth birthday was a day both he and Will always remembered. Mr. Wright's work for *The Religious Telescope* used to take him traveling quite often. On one of his journeys he found a toy that he thought would be just the thing for Orv. It looked a bit like a top, but it was a top with a difference. It was a gyroscope. Orv was delighted with his present, and his brothers were fascinated by it.

School Truant

Soon after his fifth birthday Orville was sent to kindergarten. After breakfast every day he went off, returning promptly after school hours. He always reported that he was doing fine. All went well until one day Susan Wright went along to the kindergarten to ask if Orv really was making good progress.

To her surprise the teacher said: "I thought you'd decided to keep him at home – I haven't seen him since the first few days".

Where was Orv? His mother soon found out. Bored with school, Orv had been sneaking off to see his friend, Edwin Henry Sines, who was the same age and lived two doors away on Hawthorne Street. Orv used to watch the clock carefully so that he could return home at the time he was expected.

However, Orv didn't get into too much trouble, because he and Ed had been playing with an old sewing machine which Mrs. Sines had put out in the shed. The boys had been taking the machine to pieces and trying to mend it. Mrs. Wright always encouraged her sons' interest in mechanics, so she decided not to punish Orv. But he had to go back to kindergarten right away.

Left: Orville proudly shows Kate his birthday present. The gyroscope was very important for Will and Orv because it stimulated their interest in science.

Below: Orv and Ed trying to make the old sewing machine work again. Orv's efforts saved him from punishment for playing hookey from school.

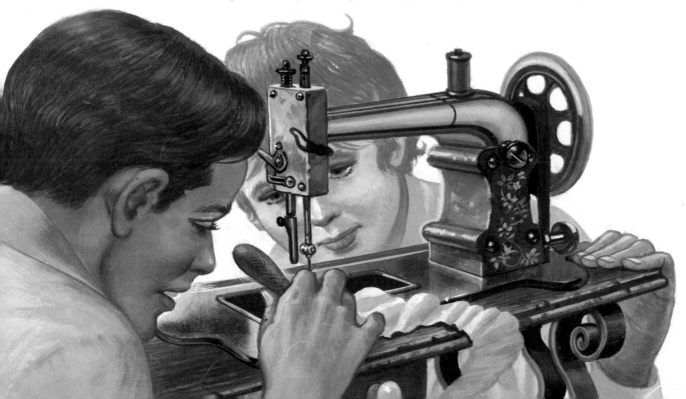

Orville collected heaps of old bones, hoping to make a lot of money by selling them to a fertilizer factory. The venture ended in a great disappointment, but it was typical of Orville's determination to persevere with an idea.

Any Old Bones?

Orv's mechanical interests – and his love of candy – were a constant drain on his pocket. One day he hit on the ideal way to earn more money. There was a local factory making fertilizer out of old bones. Orv and a friend decided they would collect a load of old bones and make a lot of money. They trudged all round the neighborhood, asking people if they had any bones. They found more on rubbish dumps and in back alleys.

After several days' hard work the two boys piled a small wagon high with bones and set off to the factory to make their fortunes. But a big disappointment was in store for them. The man who bought bones at the factory looked at the load, sized it up, and said:

"I'll give you three cents."

It wasn't the fortune they were expecting. But three cents bought them quite a lot of candy to eat while they were working, or fishing in the nearby pond.

Moving House

Orville didn't stay long at the kindergarten. A few months later a big change came about for the Wright family. The Reverend Milton Wright, who had been a minister of the United Brethren Church for 27 years, was appointed a bishop. This meant that he had different work to do, and also that he would have to move.

The family's new home was on Adam Street, Cedar Rapids, Iowa. This was much further west than the boys had ever been before. Dayton was only about 60 miles from the places where the Wrights had lived in Indiana. But Cedar Rapids was beyond the Mississippi River, 400 miles from Dayton. Bishop Wright did not sell his house in Dayton. He leased it to tenants.

THE TOY HELICOPTER

The toy helicopter was invented by a young Frenchman, Alphonse Pénaud, who made many model flying machines in the 1870s. He was the first person to use rubber bands to power his models. They have been used for model planes ever since.

Eleven-year-old Wilbur tried to build a toy helicopter of his own. He wanted to make a bigger model than the store-bought one, but his wouldn't fly because it didn't have enough power.

The Helicopter

Bishop Wright's new responsibilities meant more journeys for him. One day he came back from his travels with a present for Wilbur and Orville. He threw the gift up in the air, and the boys rushed to catch it. But the toy didn't fall right away. It soared up to the ceiling and hovered there for some seconds before it came down. It was a helicopter, made of bamboo and paper and driven by a wound-up rubber band.

Wilbur was fascinated by the toy helicopter his father gave them. He made another double the size, but it would not fly. He did not realize that the bigger machine needed not twice but eight times the power to lift it into the air.

THE EXPERIMENTER
A letter written by Orville to his absent father in April 1881 shows that he was already trying scientific experiments:
Dear Father
I got your letter today. My teacher said I was a good boy today. We have 45 in our room. The other day I took a machine can, filled it with water, then I put it on the stove. I waited a little while and the water came squirting out of the top about a foot. The water in the river was up in the cracker factory about half a foot. There is a good deal water on the Island. The old cat is dead.
Your son
Orville

Orville made kites to earn himself some money. Neither he nor Wilbur had yet thought about the possibility of powered flight. Their ambition to build a heavier-than-air flier came much later in life.

Moving Up and Moving On

Will spent a lot of his time reading. The Wright household always had plenty of books in it, and the boys were encouraged to use them. Even Orv, at nine years old, pestered his teachers to move him up to a higher class where he would have more interesting books to read.

Both boys did well at school but in 1881 they had to leave. Things were not good for the Wright family: Mrs. Susan Wright was far from well. So, after only three years at Cedar Rapids, Bishop Wright moved his family back to Indiana. They went to the small industrial city of Richmond because Susan's sister lived there, and Mrs. Wright needed to be near her.

One for the Ministry, One for the Money

Soon after the Wrights moved to Richmond, Wilbur was admitted as a full member of the United Brethren Church. He was 13 years old and thinking of following his father and studying for the ministry.

About this time Orville took up making kites as a hobby. His schoolmates clamored to buy the kites, and so Orv was able to make some money. He made even more by collecting scrap metal and selling it to a local dealer.

As Orv grew older, he and Will began to work more closely together on their projects. In a barn attached to the house they built a lathe for turning wood, more than two yards long, and driven by a treadle. Will thought it would run better if it had ball bearings, so he made some from two metal rings and some clay marbles. As soon as Orv started treadling, the marbles broke up and the whole barn began to shake. But it wasn't the lathe that was making it shake – a small tornado had struck Richmond.

The Great W. J. and M. Circus

Gansey Johnson was the boy next door. His father kept a collection of stuffed birds and animals in his barn. One day when Orville was playing with Gansey in the barn, he had a bright idea. These animals could be put to good use, especially as one of them was a huge grizzly bear.

"Let's give a circus in the barn!" he said to Gansey. Orv spoke with confidence because he had already put on a circus with another boy who had a Shetland pony.

Gansey agreed, and the two boys took another friend, Harry Morrow, as a third partner. They based the name of the circus on the initials of their surnames, and proudly announced "The Great W. J. and M. Circus".

Will undertook to organize the publicity. He wrote a glowing piece for the local paper about the circus, and the parade that would precede the performance.

As a result a large crowd gathered to watch. The parade was led by Orv and Gansey on their "iron horses" – old bicycles. (Harry missed the show – his parents had taken him away on vacation.) On wagons drawn by a crowd of boys were some of the stuffed birds and the great grizzly bear. The bear seemed larger than ever next to "Davy Crockett", Gansey's five-year-old brother Griswold.

Admission to the barn was five cents (three cents for people under three years old). It was packed, with more children clamoring to come in.

Dozens of citizens of Richmond, Indiana, turned out to watch the parade for "The Great W. J. and M. Circus". They were attracted by the piece Wilbur had written for the local paper describing the strange birds from all over the world, the pioneer hero Davy Crockett, and the proprietors on "iron horses" who would be taking part in the show!

The Young Athlete

When Wilbur was 17 and Orville 13, Bishop Wright's work took him back to Dayton, and in due course the family settled happily back into their old home on Hawthorne Street. Will was just about to graduate from high school in Richmond, but he did not feel like going back there to collect his diploma – neither he nor Orv ever set much store by certificates. Instead Will decided to take special courses in Greek and trigonometry at Steele High School in Dayton. He planned to go on to Yale Divinity School to study for the ministry.

At this time Will was tall and wiry and a first-class gymnast. He took part in all sports, especially baseball, football and hockey.

During a match between Wilbur's school and a team of officers' sons from a nearby army depot, an opponent swung his stick wildly and smashed it into Wilbur's face. He was badly hurt, and for a long time afterwards had to stay home as a semi-invalid.

When he recovered Wilbur had to look after his mother, who had been growing weaker from tuberculosis. He waited on her, and helped her up and down stairs. Bishop Wright later said that Wilbur's devoted care had prolonged his mother's life by two years.

A few months later Will had a nasty accident. During an ice hockey match a carelessly wielded stick hit him in the face. It severely injured his mouth and knocked out a lot of teeth. With care, his injuries healed, and dentures replaced the missing teeth. But the accident left Will weak, apparently with heart trouble.

Sick Nurse

Will became convinced he was going to die young. He gave up his ambitions and spent his time at home, mostly reading. And soon he was needed at home: Susan Wright, who had nursed and encouraged him after his accident, was now ill with tuberculosis. It was Will's turn to nurse her, carrying her up and down stairs. She spent most of her last two years in bed until she died at the age of 61. All this time Will, in the words of his eldest brother, Reuchlin, was "cook and chambermaid".

The Young Publisher

By this time Reuchlin was married. Lorin and Will were members of an athletic and social club, the "Ten Boys Club". Will, the youngest, was secretary. He did not trust his heart enough to take part in athletics any more.

About the time of Will's accident, Orv was beginning his new schooldays in Dayton with a protest. He had completed sixth grade at Richmond, but had no certificate to prove it. His new teachers wanted him to go into the sixth grade in

Orv and his friend Ed Sines built up a thriving business with their printing presses. But when Orv, with Will's help, started a newspaper he found that it was a lot of hard work for little money.

Dayton for another year, but Orv complained so strongly that he was allowed to enter the seventh grade. He did so well that he was soon promoted to the eighth grade.

A Midget Newspaper

Orv was delighted to be back with his old friend Ed Sines. The two boys found they had both become interested in printing, and soon they set up the "firm" of Sines & Wright. They were helped by Lorin and Wilbur, who gave them a small printing press, and Bishop Wright, who bought them some type. With this equipment Sines & Wright produced a tiny newspaper for their classmates. They called it *The Midget*, but Bishop Wright saw it and banned it. Quite probably the teachers would not have liked some of the articles!

In Business

In due course the partners acquired some more type and went into the jobbing business – that is, printing such things as handbills and posters. Ed soon sold his share of the business to Orv, but continued to work for him as an employee. Meanwhile Orv built himself a larger press, using an old marble tombstone as a bed. To learn more about printing he took a vacation job two summers running at a Dayton printing works.

With Will's help Orv built an even bigger press, and started a four-page weekly newspaper, the *West Side News*. Will, who was by now feeling better, became the editor and wrote a large part of the paper. The paper did so well that Orville decided to leave school before graduating. He and Will then converted the *West Side News* into a four-page evening paper, *The Evening Item*. It ran for just four months.

VERSE TRIBUTE
On the wall of Orville's printing shop a friend chalked this little poem:
Orville Wright is out of sight
 In the printing business;
No other mind is half so bright
 As his'n is.
That friend was Paul Laurence Dunbar, the son of a former Kentucky slave. Dunbar later became famous as a poet and novelist.

The Bicycle Business

A new invention from Europe gave the Wright brothers a new interest. It was the so-called safety bicycle, the kind now used with both wheels the same size, instead of one big and one small. Orville and Wilbur each bought bikes, and decided to open a bicycle shop to take advantage of the new craze. For a time they kept on the printing business, with Ed Sines doing most of the work there.

The new safety bicycles became popular in the 1890s, and Will and Orv soon found themselves very busy in their bicycle shop. They began making their own machines, and had to move to larger premises three times.

Otto Lilienthal (1848-1896) flying one of his gliders. He designed them after studying the way birds fly. He made several hundred flights in gliders he built himself. He died when the glider he was flying turned over in mid-flight.

The bicycle shop, with a repair shop included, was on West Third Street, Dayton, just across the road from Orville's printing shop. It proved a great success, and the brothers had to move to larger premises three times in four years. Soon they started making their own bikes from parts they brought in. They had three brand names – the Van Cleve, the St. Clair, and the Wright Special which was considerably cheaper than the others.

Lilienthal's Glider

Building, fixing and selling bicycles kept the brothers busy, but it was not a career that appealed to Will. He was looking for something new to invent.

Then one day Will came across a magazine article about a German engineer, Otto Lilienthal, who had made a machine in which he could glide through the air.

The Young Inventors

THE SHY LAD
Before his accident Will had a girl-friend, a classmate at Steele High School. But after it he seems to have become shy with any girls of his own age.

He got on well with older women, perhaps because they reminded him of the mother he spent so much time looking after.

Later, when he and Orville were hard at work on their airplane, Will used to say "I can't support a wife and a flying machine, too".

Will thought that Lilienthal's ideas on controlling his glider wouldn't work. Sure enough, one day he read that Lilienthal had crashed and been killed. At the time Orv was seriously ill with typhoid fever. As soon as he was better Will began to discuss with him his new dream: to make a machine that really would fly under its own power, controlled by a human pilot.

Flight Control
Will watched birds flying, and he remembered the kites that Orv used to make. He realized that with the right shaped wing the air could lift a flying machine, just as it could lift a kite. Putting in a motor to drive a flying machine seemed the least of their worries. The big problem was how to control the machine in the air.

The brothers set about the task methodically. First, they read everything that had been written about flight. Then they designed and built a glider, big enough to carry a man. To experiment with it they took the machine in parts to the tiny hamlet of Kitty Hawk in North Carolina. There, on a wide sandy beach, there was plenty of space to practice flying – and no one to watch them. The control system they eventually adopted was warping, or twisting, the wings to maneuver the aircraft.

Will and Orv made some of their early experiments by flying a glider rather like a kite – at the end of a series of ropes, with which they tried to control its flight.

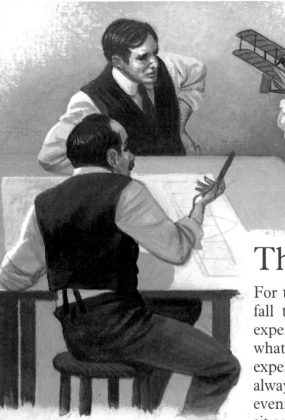

OCTAVE CHANUTE
Octave Chanute was a French-born American rail engineer. He took up the study of flight when he was 64 years old, and made many successful glides. He lived until 1910, long enough to see flying become a real success.

The First Fliers

For three years the brothers traveled to Kitty Hawk in the fall to try out their gliders. Back home in Dayton they experimented with new models, and talked endlessly about what to do next. Will was the driving force in all their experiments, but he was terribly absent-minded. Orv was always full of fun, teasing friends and relatives. In the evening, after work in the bicycle shop, the brothers would sit on either side of the fire at 7 Hawthorne Street, arguing. Kate, now a schoolteacher, used to get quite cross with them because of the noise they made.

On Kill Devil Hill

The brothers had begun their glider experiments in 1900, as soon as the busy summer season of work in the bicycle shop was over. After flying their glider like a kite, tethered by a rope, they made several short free flights with it from a huge sand mound known as Kill Devil Hill. Then they returned to Dayton to plan the next attempt.

When they talked things over in the evening Will and Orv used to argue fiercely. After a long pause in the argument one would say "T'isn't either." The other would retort "Tis too!" Kate used to get quite cross with them for the noise they made – but she supported them loyally.

26

Octave Chanute flying one of his gliders.

SAMUEL LANGLEY
The rival the Wright brothers most feared was Professor Samuel Langley, an American astronomer who had made some flying model aircraft. But Langley's two attempts to build a powered man-carrying plane ended in disaster. On both occasions the catapulted machine failed to rise and plunged into the Potomac River in Virginia.

The following year they went back to Kill Devil Hill with a new, improved glider. They left their bicycle business in the hands of an engineer, Charles Taylor, who did most of the work in it for the next eight years. This time they had some help and advice from Octave Chanute, an engineer who had made many experiments with gliders.

As a result of that season's work Wilbur decided that the calculations for wing shapes used by Lilienthal, Chanute and other experimenters were wrong. So Will built a small wind tunnel and tested model wings in it, ending up with sheets of figures about the way wings of various shapes behaved in the air.

Samuel Langley's "Aerodrome" – the name he gave to one of his powered aircraft. It plunged straight into the Potomac River when launched.

27

Success – at Last

Opposite: One of the Wright brothers' pioneer glider flights. The pilot lay prone to control the aircraft.

Below: Will with his home-made wind tunnel, in which the brothers tested model wings to see how they behaved in air currents.

In 1902 the brothers returned to Kill Devil Hill with a new glider, and this time they made glides of up to 180 yards, learning by experience how to control the machine in the air. Now, Will decided, they were ready to put an engine in the machine.

The First Flight

The following year saw them back with a new machine, The Flyer. It had a gasoline engine, which they had built themselves because they could not buy one that was light enough. They were ready to try for the world's first flight in a power-driven, heavier-than-air machine.

After an unsuccessful attempt on December 14th, with Will at the controls, success came on December 17th. Orv made the first flight into a strong head wind. It covered just 37 yards. The brothers made three more flights that day. The last, with Will on board, covered 260 yards.

The brothers had achieved their aim. Only five other people witnessed their triumph – men from the lifeboat station. Afterwards they sent a simple telegram to their father modestly describing their achievement; it ended "inform press home Christmas".

High Fliers

Will and Orv made many more experiments in a large field near Dayton, called Huffmann's Pasture. They built a new machine, Flyer 2. Now they were teaching themselves how to fly. After six months they could keep flying for several miles, turn and land successfully. In 1905 they offered their machine for sale, with flying lessons, to the U.S. War Department, and also to European countries.

The Lonely Pioneer

Negotiations with the governments of the United States, Britain and France lasted for several years. Finally, in 1909, the brothers received a $30,000 check from the U.S. Army for one of their aircraft. Other deals with countries in Europe brought their fortune up to nearly $250,000 – a very large sum in those days. They formed a company to make aircraft, and seemed set to become millionaires.

Then in 1912 Will died of typhoid fever. Orv, now a lonely pioneer, carried on with the business for three years. But it was not the same without Will's help and encouragement. So Orv sold the business and devoted the rest of his life to private experimental work in aviation.

Wilbur (left) and Orville Wright in the days of their success. The brothers usually wore formal clothes even when testing their flying machines.

Important Events in the Wright Brothers' Lives

1867 April 16: Wilbur born.
1869 Move to Dayton, Ohio.
1871 August 19: Orville born.
1874 August 19: Katharine (Kate) born.
1876 Orville goes to kindergarten.
Alexander Graham Bell invents the telephone.
1877 Milton Wright becomes a bishop.
1878 Move to Cedar Rapids.
1879 Thomas Edison invents the electric light bulb.
1881 Move to Richmond, Indiana.
1884 Return to Dayton.
1885 Will injured in ice hockey match.
Orv and Ed Sines start printing business.
First motor-cars made.
1886 Orv and Ed try to start school newspaper.
'Ten Boys Club' founded.
1887 Susan Wright taken ill. Orv builds printing press.
1888 Orv and Will build a bigger press.
1889 March: Orv and Will start the *West Side News.*
April: *The Evening Item.*
July: Susan Wright dies.
August: Paper closes.
1892 Will and Orv buy safety bicycles.
December: Wrights open a bicycle shop at 1005 West Third Street, Dayton.
1893 Move to bigger shop at 1034 West Third Street.

1894 Brothers start an occasional magazine called *Snapshots.*
1895 Shop is moved to 22 South Williams Street. Guglielmo Marconi invents wireless.
1896 Wrights begin making their own bicycles.
Orv seriously ill.
Death of Otto Lilienthal.
1898 Printing shop closed.
1899 Brothers make a biplane kite.
1900 Wrights test first glider at Kitty Hawk.
1901 Wind tunnel tests; second glider built.
1902 Third glider tested.
1903 Samuel Langley fails in attempts to fly.
Wrights build the *Flyer.* December 17: make first powered flights.
1905 Bishop Wright retires.
Build third machine which flies 24 miles in 38 minutes.
1908 Orville crashes; he is injured and his passenger, Lt. Thomas Selfridge, dies.
1909 Wrights sell their first planes.
Louis Blériot flies across the English Channel.
1912 Wilbur dies of typhoid.
1914-18 World War I.
1915 Orville sells business and retires.
1917 Bishop Wright dies.
1919 First transatlantic flight.
1939-45 World War II.
1948 Orville dies.

Index